★ SPORTS GREATS ★

TOP 10 BLOOPERS IN BASEBALL

Jamal Hinnant

Enslow
PUBLISHING

Published in 2016 by Enslow Publishing, LLC
101 W. 23rd Street, Suite 240, New York, NY 10011

Library of Congress Cataloging-in-Publication Data
Names: Hinnant, Jamal.
Title: Top 10 bloopers in baseball / Jamal Hinnant.
Description: New York : Enslow Publishing, 2016. | Series: Sports greats | Includes index.
Identifiers: ISBN 9780766073906 (pbk.) | ISBN 9780766073913 (6 pack) | ISBN 9780766073920 (library bound)
Subjects: LCSH: Baseball--United States--Miscellanea--Juvenile literature. | Baseball--Juvenile literature.
Classification: LCC GV867.5 H56 2016 | DDC 796.357--dc23

Printed in the United States of America

To Our Readers: We have done our best to make sure all website addresses in this book were active and appropriate when we went to press. However, the author and the publisher have no control over and assume no liability for the material available on those websites or on any websites they may link to. Any comments or suggestions can be sent by e-mail to customerservice@enslow.com.

Photos Credits: Cover, p. 1 Ron Kuntz Collection/Diamond Images/Getty Images (José Canseco); p. 5 Michael Zagaris/Oakland Athletics/Getty Images Sport/Getty Images; p. 7 Ronald C. Modra/Sports Imagery/Getty Images Sport/Getty Images; p. 8 Buyenlarge/Archive Photos/Getty Images; pp. 11, 15 Rich Pilling/Getty Images Sport/Getty Images; p. 12 Jon Durr/Getty Images Sport/Getty Images; p. 16 David Banks/Getty Images Sport/Getty Images; p. 19 Richey Miller/Cal Sport Media/Newscom; pp. 20, 28, 32 ©AP Images; p. 23 Jamie Squire/Getty Images Sport/Getty Images; p. 24 Hannah Foslien/Getty Images Sport/Getty Images; p. 27 Pedro Portal/Miami Herald/Tribune News Service/Getty Images; p. 31 Joe Robbins/Getty Images Sport/Getty Images; p. 35 Jason O. Watson/Getty Images Sport/Getty Images; p. 36 Bill Greene/The Boston Globe/Getty Images; p. 39 Phil Huber/Sports Illustrated/Getty Images, p. 40 Ron Kuntz Collection/Diamond Images/Getty Images; p. 43 Elsa/Getty Images Sport/Getty Images; p. 44 Bob Levey/Getty Images Sport/Getty Images.

★ Contents ★

★ Introduction ★

The Major League Baseball Association (MLBA) signs contracts worth millions of dollars each year. Teams shell out so much cash because they are in search of the best players in the league. They want the best hitters, the fastest runners, and players who do well under pressure. Since the start of Major League Baseball in 1869, however, we have learned that sometimes even the best players make big mistakes.

Unfortunately for the athletes, every fall and missed catch, every bad throw, every time a player runs into a wall (or worse), or every time players run into each other is recorded for all to see. Fans get to watch in horror as their favorite team suffers from the mistakes. Even if it's the team they love, fans cannot stop laughing at the bloopers as they make the headlines in papers, top stories on the nightly news, and funny collections of videos online. Just like the time Minnesota Twins outfielder Kyle Waldrop lost his shoe rallying toward third base, in the fourth inning of a minor league game against the Los Angeles Dodgers in 2015.

Waldrop hit a base hit toward deep right center field. He ran full speed around second base on the way to third when it happened. His shoe went flying off behind him. He didn't stop running though; he stayed focused and managed to leg out a triple. He slid to third just barely making it to the base before the ball was thrown to third. The second base umpire picked up Waldrop's shoe for him, laughing while he walked to third base to return it to him. Although he didn't make our countdown, it was a pretty funny blooper.

The Oakland Athletics' Billy Burns and Josh Reddick crash and drop the ball in a 2015 game against the San Diego Padres.

Sometimes the most amazing bloopers turn out to be amazing plays, leading to amazing games. The level of focus and athleticism it takes for a player to keep his composure raises the bar for his teammates to continue the drive with the same intensity. When the athlete who is at the center of the blooper completes the play, the mistake is considered saved. But it's still a moment fans will never forget. There are many accidents on record, but this resource covers some of the funniest bloopers in Major League Baseball history.

Before we get started, we have to acknowledge a different kind of blooper. And this one may be a fan favorite. While at the games cheering on the teams they love, sometimes a bit of a blooper has splashed into a few fans' drinks: a foul ball! With the excitement of the moment and thousands of fans cheering them on, there's a growing movement. The fan finishes his or her drink with the ball still inside, all while on national television. These fans become stars for a moment, and they get the best souvenir at a Major League Baseball game: a baseball.

★ Lloyd Moseby ★

Team:	*Toronto Blue Jays*
Position:	*Center fielder*
Number:	*15*
Blooper:	*Stole second base twice in the same play*

We have all heard the stories. Children who are learning sports accidently run the wrong way. Meanwhile all the adults shout and wave to the confused child to run the other way. These stories usually end in laughs and ice cream after the game. Mistakes happen. But one time a major league player actually stole second base, and then first base, and then stole second base again—all within the same play!

This list of bloopers wouldn't be complete without Lloyd Anthony Moseby. Moseby was also known as "Shaker," a name that came from high school, when he could get around players who attempted to defend him on the basketball court. Moseby graduated from Oakland High School in California. In 1978, the amateur team the Toronto Blue Jays drafted him as their first pick, second overall that year. Moseby played his first Major League

Baseball game in May 1980. He was known as one of the fastest base runners, stealing more than 30 bases a season. He was also a great batter, exceeding his rookie year expectations. The span of Moseby's career consists of a .257 batting average with 869 runs, 169 home runs (HRs), 737 runs batted in (RBIs), and 280 stolen bases (SBs). In 1986, he was named an All-Star.

Lloyd Moseby was speedy, but during one game he ran back and forth between first and second base to stay safe: that's 270 feet (90 yards) just to get 90 feet (30 yd)!

Not much is recorded from the game, but here is what we know. It was a game against the Chicago White Sox, and Moseby successfully stole second base. The throw from the catcher went into center field, but shortstop Ozzie Guillen acted as if the ball had popped up. Moseby thought that he was about to cause a double out and ran back to first base instead of taking the extra base. The center fielder threw it to first, but the ball went into the dugout. Moseby quickly took advantage of the missed throw and stole second base again. By now, he had run a total of 270 feet (82 meters) just to get 90 feet (27 m)! Once he made it back to second base, he threw his hands up in disbelief.

Herman "Germany" Schaefer would bring props like cameras on the field, and once he stole first base from second . . . on purpose!

It's hard to decide if the blooper should have been placed against Moseby or against the entire White Sox defense for allowing this to happen.

There is only one other blooper where a player stole first base from second base. Herman "Germany" Schaefer was also known as "Dutch" and "the Prince." He was known to be a notorious prankster in baseball. He would do things like wear a raincoat or carry a lantern out onto the field during the game to hint to the umpire that the game should be called off because of the rain or the darkness. He stole first base from second on purpose. Because of Schaefer, a new rule was created shortly after his death. The Official Major League Baseball Code of Rules rule 7.08i declares, "After he has acquired legal possession of a base, [if] he runs the bases in reverse order for the purpose of confusing the defense or making a travesty of the game... [the] umpire shall immediately call 'Time' and declare the runner out." Schaefer's blooper changed the way Major League Baseball is played.

★ John Lester ★

Team:	*Chicago Cubs*
Position:	*Pitcher*
Number:	*34*
Blooper:	*Threw entire glove to first base for the out*

In Major League Baseball, you need wit and skill, but it's the fast reaction that saves the day for many of the big plays. It's not about what happens, but how well you recover when unexpected things happen. Later in this resource, we'll consider the swift recovery made by Cincinnati Reds pitcher Anthony DeSclafani after losing his glove. But for now, here is another example of what happens when wit, skill, action, and a whole lot of teamwork come together on a baseball field.

Before becoming a Chicago Cubs pitcher, Jon Lester graduated from Bellarmine Preparatory School in Tacoma, Washington. During his high school career, he was three-time MVP (most valuable player) and three-time All-Area selection. He was also named Gatorade State Player of the Year for Washington in 2000.

He was drafted in the second round of the 2002 Major League Baseball Draft. He played in the minors until 2005, earning impressive feats, including league-best 163 strikeouts for the Portland Sea Dogs in 2005, Eastern League Pitcher of the Year, and Red Sox Minor Pitcher of the year, and he was on the all-star team. This was all during the minors. His major league feats include three-time All-Star and two World Series championships, and he has pitched a no-hitter. This is all after he announced that he was diagnosed with lymphoma in 2005.

Although he was diagnosed with lymphoma in 2005, John Lester continued to thrive as a three-time All-Star and a two-time World Series champion. He also pitched a no-hitter.

On April 19, 2015, Jon Lester and the Chicago Cubs faced off with the San Diego Padres. It was the top of the second inning, with one man on first base; the game was tied at two each. Lester pitched a fastball to the Padres shortstop, Clint Barnes. Barnes hit a grounder directly over the pitcher's mound. This was a bad move on Barnes's part because there was already a player on first base

Fans continued to clap and cheer after Lester threw his entire glove—the ball stuck inside—to first base where Anthony Rizzo made an out.

trying to make it to second. It looked like an inning-ending double play was about to happen, but then things got a little sticky.

Lester stopped the ground ball, catching it in his glove, and turned to throw to second base, but the ball was stuck in his glove. He realized that he could not make the double play and turned his attention toward first base. Thanks to Lester's quick reaction and quick thinking, all was not lost. He bolted toward first base, removing his glove with the ball still inside. With an underhanded toss, he threw the entire glove to first baseman Anthony Rizzo. Rizzo quickly removed his glove so that he could catch Lester's glove without interference. Although Lester didn't get the double play that he wanted, the Cubs' excellent teamwork and fast actions stopped Barnes, with Rizzo tagging him out at first. Rizzo gave the glove back to Lester as they walked toward the pitcher's mound. Lester loosely carried the glove showing the ball wedged in the glove's net. He was able to remove the ball and continue pitching. In the end, the San Diego Padres outplayed Jon Lester and the Chicago Cubs 5 to 2.

On-the-field bloopers happen all the time. But surely Lester would agree that how you recover from the unexpected determines if you are a star.

★ Anthony DeSclafani ★

Team:	*Cincinnati Reds*
Position:	*Pitcher*
Number:	*28*
Blooper:	*Lost his bat and glove in the same game*

Much like any other professional sport, Major League Baseball has motivational phrases that players and teams recite. Often these phrases become the motto for the players, teams, and franchises. You may have heard, "Seven days without baseball makes one weak," or "Reaching high keeps a man on his toes." But perhaps Anthony DeSclafani should change his motto to "Hold on tight and don't let go!" He helped his team hold on to a win, but holding on to his bat and glove was a different story.

Anthony DeSclafani graduated from Colts Neck High School in Colts Neck, New Jersey. He played for the University of Florida's Gators baseball team before being drafted in the sixth round of the 2011 Major League Baseball Draft. In 2013, he was named the minor league pitcher of the year by the Marlins. He played for the minors for one more season before being traded to the Miami Marlins in 2014, when he made his major league debut. Then in December of the same year he was traded to the Cincinnati Reds. Expectations were set high for this rookie pitcher, and he's had a solid grip on it, or maybe not!

Anthony DeSclafani knows where his glove is as he poses for this photograph, but that was not always the case.

On April 14, 2015, the Cincinnati Reds were playing the Chicago Cubs. DeSclafani threw seven scoreless innings and led the Reds to victory over the Cubs with a final score of 3–2. However, humorous "rumors" circled the Internet that DeSclafani dipped his hands in butter because everything kept slipping from his grip during this game.

In the bottom of the fifth inning, Cincinnati was leading Chicago 3–0. DeSclafani tried to do his job in style with a swift behind-the-back catch. He pitched a fastball to shortstop Starlin Castro. Castro connected with a grounder directly back to the pitcher's mound when DeSclafani tried for a backhand grab and

After pitching seven scoreless innings on April 14, 2015, DeSclafani would not only leave his glove behind in a play but also dropped his bat when he was up to hit.

the glove slid off of his left hand. He did make contact with the ball, managing to stop it. With Castro sprinting to first, DeSclafani used pure reaction to complete the play. He ran to recover the ball and made the throw to first base for the out, leaving his glove behind. Cheers could be heard all throughout the stadium after the play was complete. It left DeSclafani puzzled as he adjusted his glove and continued the game.

Nothing had changed with the scores just two innings later, at the top of the seventh with one out, one ball, and one strike. Chicago pitcher Jake Arrieta threw a curveball. DeSclafani took a swing and missed, and his bat slipped right out of his hands and flew behind him. Although he had better-gripping batting gloves on, it made no difference. The bat hit the ground and flipped behind him toward the wall. Everyone erupted in laughter as he went to retrieve his bat. As for DeSclafani, he was all smiles.

★ Brian Walker ★

Team:	*Arkansas Travelers (Minor League)*
Position:	*Catcher*
Number:	*N/A*
Blooper:	*Faked getting hit by pitch*

Every professional athlete knows that skill is what makes the play, but it is finesse that creates the fans. The most famous players don't just get the job done. They also make it look good. The behind-the-back catches, the dives, the over-the-wall jumping, the home-run blocks, the running catches, the double and triple plays, the base stealing, and the out-of-the-park hits are what make baseball America's favorite sport. We love the action! We cheer when there is a successful play, boo when our team is losing, and clap with support if a player gets injured. Fans love to see athletic performance matched by a little acting, but what happens when athletes do more showing off than showing skill?

Just ask retired catcher Brian Walker, now the assistant baseball coach for the Division 1 Wichita State Shockers. Walker was drafted by the Los Angeles Angels of Anaheim in the twenty-ninth round of the 2007 Major League Baseball June Amateur Draft from the University of Arkansas. Until his retirement in 2010, he played for five minor league teams, including the Arkansas Travelers, where he was a three-time letter winner (2005–2007).

Brian Walker slugs the ball in 2008, handling the pitch a lot more professionally than he did in his 2006 blooper.

Back in spring 2006, the Ole Miss Rebels faced Brian Walker and the Arkansas Travelers. Walker was up to bat at the top of the third inning. Ole Miss was leading the game 1–0. There was one ball and two strikes, and no one at base. Brett Bukvich, Ole Miss pitcher, threw a curveball that just missed hitting Walker. Walker, batting righty, did not swing at the ball; instead, he performed what is arguably one of the biggest performances in minor league history. He dropped the bat and immediately grabbed his right arm while crouching and running away from the home plate. The pitch was outside the pocket and came close to hitting him but didn't. An Arkansas medical staff member rushed to the field to check on Walker and told him he didn't get hit. The replays

Ole Miss pitcher Brett Bukvich pitched a ball very close to Walker, who dramatically dropped his bat and fell to the ground, though he was never touched!

from every angle showed that the ball did not touch Walker but probably would have, had he swung his bat. The umpire declared it as a strike, and Walker had to continue at bat with one strike left. Bukvich pitched another strike. This time, Walker took the bait on a curveball and missed.

After being struck out, Walker pointed the bat at the umpire, which is considered a threat toward the umpire. He was immediately ejected from the game. The acting continued as Walker exploded with rage, shouting at the umpire. He snatched off his helmet and flung it on the ground. He continued shouting and also threw his bat to the ground before returning to the Arkansas dugout, where his yelling continued. Arkansas head coach Dave Van Horn argued with the umpire for the ejection call against Walker before the game continued. But the ejection stood as a fair call.

In an interview with Paul Suellentrop of the *Wichita Eagle* newspaper, Walker admitted that he overreacted. He apologized to the umpire, Nelson Graham, later that season. Walker said, "I was so fortunate to be able to get to see him again. That was something I thought was important, that I was at least able to apologize to him and let him know I felt bad."

★ Mike Moustakas ★

Team:	Kansas City Royals
Position:	Third baseman
Number:	8
Blooper:	Mental error ended the game

As with any other sport, baseball takes focus. The pace and length of the baseball game is longer than almost any other professional sport, so there is a seventh-inning stretch. In the course of such a long game, it becomes a skill to stay alert throughout nine innings. Every player's mind wanders every so often. And that's OK just as long as he pulls it together before the next big play. No one wants to let his team and the fans down by missing a play because of a mental error. They can be costly. Kansas City Royals third baseman Mike Moustakas knows this all too well.

Michael Christopher Moustakas was a four-year starter during his high school baseball career at Chatsworth High School in California. There he won four West Valley League Championships and two Los Angeles City Section CIF (California Interscholastic Federation) city titles. He was voted Player of the Year for two years straight by Cal-Hi Sports, which is a California high school sports company under ESPN that keeps rankings, recruiting information, and records in the state. During his senior year at Chatsworth, he hit 24 home runs, which set a single-season state record and a California state record at 52 total high school career home runs.

Mike Moustakas was an award-winning minor league player when he was drafted to the Kansas City Royals in 2007.

The Kansas City Royals drafted him with the second overall pick of the 2007 amateur draft. Just two years later MLB .com ranked Moustakas as the eleventh best prospect overall in all of minor league baseball. While in the minors, he raked in a bunch of awards including the 2010 Texas League Player of the Year award, the same night he broke the record for the Omaha Royals with 3 home runs and 11 RBIs in a single game.

Having a brain freeze is one thing. Having one while you're at bat, now that's enough to earn a spot on our top ten blooper list. On April 12, 2015, Moustakas with the Kansas City Royals faced off against the Minnesota Twins. It was the top of the ninth

Moustakas hits a single on April 13, 2015. The day before, instead of running to base, Moustakas froze in place, causing Twins catcher Kurt Suzuki to run into him.

inning with two outs. The Royals were trailing by one run, and the bases were empty. Moustakas hit a pop-up, but instead of running to first base, he froze in place, believing that the ball would be a foul ball. When a batter hits a pop-up, the defensive team will most commonly try to make the catch, and that's exactly what Minnesota did. Twins catcher Kurt Suzuki tried to catch it, but he bumped into Moustakas. Even though the ball hit the ground in foul territory, Moustakas was out! Laz Diaz, the umpire at home plate, called Moustakas out for interference. Official Major League Baseball rule 6.08c says that a batter is out for illegal action when he interferes with the catcher's fielding or throwing by stepping out of the batter's box or making any other movement that prevents the catcher's play at home base. "Regardless of the rulebook," says David Brown for Yahoo! Sports, "it's the oldest unwritten rule in the imaginary baseball book, and it's the best rule: When in doubt, run it out. Always. Run. It. Out." Hopefully, Moustakas will remember that rule and prevent a future blooper!

★ Dee Gordon ★

Team:	*Miami Marlins*
Position:	*Second baseman/Shortstop*
Number:	*9*
Blooper:	*Fell on the way to first base*

There is a zone that the best athletes get in when they are doing exceptionally well, as if nothing can faze them. During this time, the players are more engaged in the sport and making sharper decisions, which leads to the best outcome of the play, and ultimately the game. Every coach wants the players to be in that zone before the game starts. It allows teammates to feed off of the positive energy, helping everyone perform at top athletic ability. But some days, even the best players stumble, even in that zone.

Devaris "Dee" Gordon, second oldest son of former major league pitcher Tom Gordon, played for Avon Park High School, Seminole Community College, and Southeastern University. Then he was drafted by the Los Angeles Dodgers in the fourth round of the 2008 Major League Baseball Draft. The talent runs in his family. The Minnesota Twins drafted his half-brother, Nick Gordon, in the first round of the 2014 draft.

Every athlete has experienced days when he is not playing at his best. Fans watch as these players stumble through the game trying to make a decent play. On April 6, 2015, against the Atlanta Braves, Miami Marlins second baseman Gordon was going through that very struggle. He based only once in his four times at bat. It was the bottom of the eighth inning, and the Braves were leading the

Dee Gordon bunts on March 10, 2015. His bunt the next month would prove much more memorable, unfortunately.

Marlins 2–1. Dee Gordon was up to bat with one out. The pitch came in at 88 miles (about 142 km) per hour, slow enough for anyone to connect, even if it was a slider or curveball.

Gordon decided to sacrifice a bunt, which should have allowed him to make it to first base. His bat made contact with the ball, and he took off, sprinting to first. After about five steps, he stumbled

After a bunt, Dee Gordon took off toward first base but quickly tripped and fell flat on his face in front of the sold-out crowd.

and fell face down, sliding a few inches before coming to a complete stop. Braves pitcher Henderson Alvarez intercepted the ball. He saw that Gordon had taken a fall and took his time throwing to first base for the out. Gordon made no attempt to get up because he already knew he was out.

The game was paused for sixteen minutes in the second inning because of rain. Marlins president David Samson decided a little too late to close the retractable roof at the three-year-old Marlins Park. What made it worse for Gordon was the completely sold-out crowd. Gordon did not suffer any injuries from that play, and he walked himself to the dugout, where his team and the huge crowd enjoyed a great laugh at his expense.

Marlins general manager Mike Redmond blamed the wet dirt. "When you close that roof down, it doesn't dry," he said. "I'm sure that had a lot to do with it." To completely blame this blooper on the wet ground would have worked except no other player fell during a sprint to first base. The video of Gordon falling shows that more blame should have been placed on his bad posture than the wet field. After he laid down a nearly perfect bunt, he led into his run off balance, creating a recipe for disaster.

Justin Upton and Melvin Upton Jr.

Team:	Atlanta Braves
Positions:	Outfielders: Justin, left field, and Melvin "B.J.," center field
Numbers:	Justin 8, Melvin "B.J." 2
Blooper:	Brothers collide into each other

Baseball is widely known as a family sport. Families enjoy it as fans of the same team or as families who play the sport together. Our blooper discussion would not be complete without a family on our list. At one time, these two brothers played on the same team, both as outfielders. Justin Upton and Melvin Upton Jr. made a great duo for the Atlanta Braves although it was short lived, for only two seasons. During one of these seasons, the Upton brothers made a crashing good blooper.

Melvin Emanuel "B.J." Upton has gone by "B.J. Upton" throughout his amateur and professional career. While attending Greenbrier Christian Academy in Virginia, he was a member of the 2001 Team USA Junior National Team, the same year he won a silver medal in Cuba. He was also named a first-team All-American by Baseball America in 2002. He was the second overall pick by Tampa Bay in the 2002 Major League Baseball Draft.

A family full of talent, B.J.'s brother also made a name for himself. Justin Irving Upton was awarded the AFLAC National Player of the Year Award in 2005. He was also an All-District shortstop for Great Bridge High School in Virginia. The Diamondbacks chose Justin in the 2005 MLB draft. Justin was a first overall selection directly out of high school. He was highly desirable because he was a five-tool player. He had all the essential skills of an above-average baseball player

The Upton brothers, Justin (#8) and B.J. (#2), both play for the Atlanta Braves as outfielders.

Although it was a few years apart, the Upton brothers are officially the only two brothers in Major League Baseball history selected number one and two in the draft. They are also the first brothers to hit 20 home runs and have 20 stolen bases in a single season, making it into the **20-20** club.

B.J. Upton good-naturedly gives Justin a shove after the two of them miscommunicated and ended up crashing into one another to catch a fly ball.

The 2013 Atlanta Braves' starting roster listed both brothers. It was the second game of a doubleheader on June 18, 2013, against the New York Mets. At the top of the fifth inning, tied at zero, with two outs, Mets shortstop Omar Quintanilla was up to bat with three balls and one strike. Braves pitcher Mike Minor threw a fastball, and Quintanilla connected a fly ball to left center field. The Upton brothers both went to catch it. Replays of the video show B.J. signaling to his brother that he had the catch, but Justin was focused only on the ball. Just as B.J. snatched the catch, Justin came charging in, colliding into his brother. They both hit the ground, sending Justin into a backward tumble as he protected his glove from hitting the ground. The fans let out a moan and then the stadium roared in laughter. The brothers did not suffer any injuries from the collision. They both got up, and while walking back infield, B.J. gave his little brother a light-hearted push as they both laughed. This play kept the game tied for another scoreless inning. Although the Atlanta Braves were the first-place team with the most victories for the 2013 season, they lost both of the games that night in the doubleheader, finishing this game 6–1 behind the Mets.

★ Prince Fielder ★

Team:	*Texas Rangers*
Position:	*First baseman and designated hitter*
Number:	*84*
Blooper:	*Multiple falls*

Prince Fielder is the son of Cecil Grant Fielder, a former professional baseball player and known power hitter of the 1980s and 1990s. Prince was the first-round draft pick, seventh overall selection by the Milwaukee Brewers during the 2002 Major League Baseball Draft. He played for the minor leagues for three years before being called to his first major league game on June 13, 2005. He was used as a pinch hitter, and at the time he was the second youngest player in the league.

Since his major league debut, Prince Fielder has continued the Fielder family legacy as a revered power hitter. Prince has more than 300 home runs under his belt and only one bunt in his entire career. Although the gentle giant has made a name for himself for being strong, he is also known for his bloopers. Fielder has a wide selection of great blooper reels. Let's look at his three biggest fails.

First, there was the 2013 American League Championship Series, the best of seven play-offs with the Boston Red Sox against Fielder's team, the Detroit Tigers on October 19 at Fenway Park. During game six, at the top of the sixth inning, Fielder reached

Prince Fielder is known to be gentle . . . until it comes time to slug a baseball. At bat he's known for his mighty swing.

on a walk from Red Sox reliever Franklin Morales and moved to third on a Victor Martinez single. Johnny Peralta hit a groundball to second; Dustin Pedroia tagged the runner out and then threw the ball home. Fielder was stopped short of running home but started stutter stepping in an attempt to taunt or trick the catcher to throw the ball to third, which would have given him a chance to score. The catcher wasn't fooled. Instead he chased down Fielder, forcing him to make a quick dive back toward third base. But he belly flopped, sliding too soon, and stopped short of making it to

Fielder has a number of bloopers under his belt, including this belly flop that fell too short of third base to make him safe.

the base. He was tagged out. A few seconds went by while he lay there taking in all of the laughter around the stadium.

On opening day, April 6, 2015, against the Oakland Athletics, in the bottom of the fifth inning at Oakland Coliseum (fondly known as "O.co"), Prince Fielder did it again. The Oakland Athletics were leading the Texas Rangers in a shutout. This time Fielder was trying to field a simple pop-up ball to the side of first base. He ran for the ball and tried to make a diving catch but he fell face-first, missing the ball completely. He turned around and sat up for a few seconds. His teammate Roborto Odor retrieved the ball and helped Fielder to his feet. He couldn't help but laugh at himself as he returned to the field.

Fielder's third and most recent fall might be the worst. On June 16, 2015, the Rangers faced off against the Los Angeles Dodgers. It was the bottom of the first inning with two outs, with Kyle Blanks on first base and Fielder on second. Mitch Moreland hit a single to left field to secure all bases loaded. While rounding third, Fielder tripped and fell face-first. It turned out to be a good thing for Texas because the power throw to home plate by Andre Ethier would have easily tagged out Fielder. He ran back to third base, where he was safe. He turned and pointed to the crowd and laughed along with everyone else. His teammates did not let him live it down as they were seen smiling throughout the rest of the game. Prince Fielder's falls are among some of the more popular sports blooper viral videos of all time.

★ José Canseco ★

Team:	*Texas Rangers*
Position:	*Center fielder*
Number:	*33*
Blooper:	*Ball bounces off of his head for the home run*

This next blooper may have happened only a few times in all of MLB history. Younger baseball fans may know about San Diego Padre Wil Myers's infamous blooper against Houston Astro Evan Gattis's bat. By the time Myers got to the fence, he was able to get a glove on the ball, but he couldn't pull the catch. The ball bounced off of his glove, hitting him in the head before bouncing over the fence for the home run! The first time this kind of blooper happened rewinds the years back to 1993. It happens to be from a player who was arguably one of the best in the major leagues at the time: José Canseco.

José Canseco Jr. relocated from Cuba to Florida with his family and identical twin brother, Ozzie, when they were infants. José and Ozzie grew up in Miami and attended Coral Park High School. Canseco was drafted in the 1982 Major League Baseball

Draft. Ozzie was drafted into the MLB four years later. José gained the nickname "Parkway José" for his long home runs that went close to Memorial Parkway behind Joe Davis Stadium. Canseco was a six-time All-Star with an impressive list of awards. He was a four-time Silver Slugger Award recipient and two-time home run champion. In 1985, Canseco won the Baseball America Minor League Player of the Year Award. In 1986, he won AL Rookie of the Year, the same year he made his debut for the Oakland Athletics. In 1988, he recorded 42 home runs and 40 steals. He was the first player to hit the 40-40 mark in a single season. This is just a small sampling of his awards.

José Canseco hits so many long homers that he is known as "Parkway José."

Canseco is known for his powerful home runs. (In fact, he and Mark McGuire are fondly known as the "Bash Brothers.") But he is forever immortalized in baseball history for a more comical

On May 26, 1993, Canseco was going for the out when instead of catching the fly ball, it hit him right in the head!

defensive play. On May 26, 1993, Canseco and the Texas Rangers were playing the Cleveland Indians when one of the best bloopers in MLB history took place. Carlos Martinez, the Indians infielder, hit a deep fly ball to the warning track, the patch of dirt near the right field wall. José Canseco looked like he was going to be able to make the out, but instead of making the catch, the ball hit Canseco square in the head! It bounced off of his noggin and flew over the fence. Everyone burst out in laughs, even his teammate, outfielder David Hulse, who made it to the wall just after the ball bounced off of Canseco's head and had to explain what happened to a clearly confused Canseco. Hulse tried to suppress his giggles the whole time as they walked back infield. This is not what the coach means when he tells the players to use their heads.

On May 26, 2014, Canseco wrote a post on his Twitter account, showing that he still finds humor in his error. The tweet reads, "I see today is 21st anniversary of the ball of[f] my head game. Poor Ball will never be the same."

★ Jonathan Villar ★

Team:	Houston Astros
Position:	Shortstop
Number:	34
Blooper:	Slid into a player's backside

Next up to bat is a famous blooper that no one saw coming. It sure turned out to be a face full of funny. You might call this one a real stinker.

The Houston Astros were having one of their worst seasons ever. They were carrying the worst win–loss record in Major League Baseball, with a total of 99 losses in 2013. The Astros wanted to turn things around at their next game on September 17, against the Cincinnati Reds, but their plans failed. Apparently being a member of the team that just reached their one hundredth loss of the season wasn't enough. By the end of the game, Astros shortstop Jonathan Villar had fans yelling out, "You stink!"

Jonathan Rafael Villar Roque was born and raised in the Dominican Republic. The Philadelphia Phillies signed him as an international free agent in 2008. Baseball America named Villar the ninety-fourth best prospect in 2011. He was traded that same year to the Houston Astros after a year in the minors. Villar made his major league debut in July 2013 and has been an asset to the team because of his speed and accuracy. With only two seasons under his belt, he already had career stats of 39 stolen bases and 42 RBIs.

On September 17, 2013, the Houston Astros faced off against the Cincinnati Reds. It was the bottom of the first inning, and the Reds had already given up four runs to zero. Villar was up to bat against Astros pitcher Mike Leake and sent a piping hot curveball off of his bat bouncing past second base. It was a leadoff single, meaning that he was the first batter up for his team, but Villar tried to stretch his single base hit into a double and was thrown out in a most embarrassing way. The ball was stopped by Cincinnati outfielder Shin-Soo Choo, who threw it to second baseman Brandon Phillips to make the play.

Shortstop Jonathan Villar has made a name for himself with his speed and accuracy.

On September 17, 2013, Villar was trying for a double when he went sliding into the rear end of Cincinnati's second baseman, Brandon Phillips.

Phillips bent down and made the tag between his legs, just as Villar came sliding in toward second, crashing face-first into Phillips's bottom. He had a long walk back to the dugout after having a face full of rear end, all because he decided to stretch what could have been a successful single.

After the game, Brandon Phillips posted his feelings about the play on Twitter: "Normally after a W[in], I'm feeling great! But after what happen[ed] to me during the game, all I can say is, THAT ... WAS FUNNY! #ButtTag."

A lot of time goes into developing a great baseball player. Professionals can spend years developing in the minor leagues before they earn their spots on the major teams. This is a time for mistakes as the players learn to be consistent and avoid errors. Only the top prospects actually weave their way into the spotlight because they are willing to do whatever it takes to win. Their leave-it-all-on-the-field mentality makes great games and unforgettable bloopers.

★ Glossary ★

batting gloves—Form-fitting gloves that allow baseball players to have a better grip on the bat.

blooper—An error or funny moment that is usually caught on camera.

bunt—A baseball offensive technique where the batter loosely holds the bat over the pitcher's mound and lightly hits a pitched ball so that the ball will travel a short distance, usually allowing time for a base run.

ejection—A call made by the umpire that disqualifies a person from the game due to a violation of MLB rules.

five-tool player—A baseball player (other than the pitcher) who excels in five categories: hitting for average, power hitting, base running skills and speed, throwing ability, and fielding abilities.

40-40 mark—When a baseball player hits 40 home runs and has 40 stolen bases in a single season.

franchise—A team and its operating organization in a professional sports league.

interference—A call made by an umpire because of an act by a member of the team at bat that interferes with or hinders the defensive team attempting to make the play.

international free agent—Player that is drafted into MLB and lives outside of the United States, Canada, or Puerto Rico.

Major League Baseball Draft—The selection of players by Major League Baseball teams.

Official Major League Baseball Code of Rules—A list of rules and regulations that govern the sport of baseball.

pinch hitter—A substitute batter.

retractable roof—A modern feature in newer baseball stadiums where the electronic roof of the stadium can be closed or opened, usually determined by the weather.

seventh-inning stretch—A baseball tradition that takes place after the first half of the seventh inning, allowing the fans a chance to stretch; it also gives the players a small break.

20-20 club—Baseball batters who have gained 20 stolen bases and 20 home runs in a single season.

viral video—A video that is popular through Internet sharing.

warning track—The patch of dirt that runs along the baseball outfield, just before the home run fence or wall.

★ Further Reading ★

Books

Gutman, Bill. *Baseball Bloopers* (World's Funniest Errors). Mahwah, NJ: Troll Communications LLC, 2003.

Martirano, Ron. *Baseball: Great Records, Weird Happenings, Odd Facts, Amazing Moments & Other Cool Stuff.* Watertown, MA: Imagine Pub Inc., 2010.

Savage, Jeff. *Prince Fielder* (Amazing Athletes). Minneapolis, MN: Lerner Publications Co., 2013.

Tocher, Timothy, and Stacy Curtis. *Odd Ball: Hilarious, Unusual, & Bizarre Baseball Moments.* New York, NY: Marshall Cavendish Children, 2011.

Websites

Baseball Comedy

http://www.pikore.com/best.baseball.bloopers

Keep the laughter going and stay current with daily video uploads of baseball comedy from Little Leagues to the majors and everything in between.

40 Most Hilarious Bloopers in Baseball History

http://bleacherreport.com/articles/818385-40-most-hilarious-bloopers-in-baseball-history

A look back at the funniest moments in baseball history, all in one place.

This Week In Baseball 20 Years of Unforgettable Plays & Bloopers in MLB

http://tune.pk/video/2777710/this-week-in-baseball-20-years-of-unforgettable-plays-amp-bloopers

Prepare to be tickled by this amazing compilation of mistakes in baseball.

★ INDEX ★